D0058351

Hunger in Paradise

Hunger in Paradise

By **Rasmus Ankersen**

Hunger in Paradise

By Rasmus Ankersen © Turbulenz Publishing

Cover photos: Gudmund Thai

Cover design: Danni Riddertoft

Content layout: Jan Birkefeldt

Printed by Specialtrykkeriet Arco

Printed in Denmark 2018

ISBN: 978-0-9956162-0-2

Table of Contents

Lead Author

Rasmus Ankersen

Rasmus Ankersen is a bestselling author, entrepreneur, speaker on performance development and a trusted advisor to businesses and athletes around the world.

In 2012 Rasmus published The Gold Mine Effect, in which he explores how some countries and cities develop a disproportionate amount of top talent.

Rasmus is also the chairman of FC Midtjylland, his childhood football club in Denmark, and a director of the English club Brentford FC. Both are known as some of the world's most innovative football clubs, especially recognised for their use of big data to drive decision-making.

How to contact Rasmus:
Website: www.rasmusankersen.com

For speaking enquiries please contact Alyson
Pendlebury:
Email: alyson@rasmusankersen.com
Phone: +44 7830 677 994

To address questions and comments about the book
directly to Rasmus please write to:
rasmus@rasmusankersen.com

Find Rasmus on social media:
LinkedIn: www.linkedin.com/in/rasmusankersen
Twitter: www.twitter.com/RasmusAnkersen

Co-Author

Henrik Hyldgaard

Henrik Hyldgaard is a strategic thinker and a specialist in transforming successful companies in a state of complacency into hungry and competitive brands.

Since 2013 Henrik has been working on implementing the principles of "Hunger In Paradise" in successful companies. The CEOs guide to Hunger In Paradise can be downloaded for free at his website.

How to contact Henrik
Website: www.henrikhyldgaard.com

For speaking and consulting enquiries please contact:
Email: hh@henrikhyldgaard.com

Find Henrik on social media:
LinkedIn: www.linkedin.com/in/henrikhyldgaard
Twitter: www.twitter.com/HenrikHyld

From Greatness to Irrelevance

How success sows the seeds of failure

Do you remember this?

It is a Nokia 3310, once hailed as the world's best mobile phone. After its launch in September 2000 it sold over 126 million units worldwide. Back then, when people bought a mobile phone they invariably bought a Nokia.

On most key parameters the Nokia 3310 was superior to its competitors. The battery lasted a week. It was the first phone that allowed you to write text messages longer than a few sentences. You could even play Snake II on it.

But most of all the Nokia 3310 was famous for being indestructible. In drop tests it made other phones look like porcelain. As the saying goes in the mobile industry: if someone drops an iPhone the screen breaks, but if someone drops a Nokia 3310 the floor breaks. It was thrown off tall buildings, run over by lorries, smashed by hammers, shot at, and even set on fire. And it survived more of those trials than anyone would expect. In many ways, the 3310 embodied what Nokia stood for as a brand: resilience.

It was iconic products like the 3310 that turned Nokia into one of the world's biggest companies and a case study for business schools everywhere. But there is a more tragic side to the story. Having continued to dominate the mobile industry for the first decade of the 2000s Nokia gradually began to lose momentum, and within a few years the company had completely lost its mojo. From being worth $150 billion and having around half of the smartphone market share at the end of 2007, Nokia's fall was so sharp that by the final quarter of 2012 its market share was just 2.9%, and a year later the ruins of its mobile business was sold to Microsoft.

And the Nokia 3310? Well, today the indestructible phone rests in peace in the gadget graveyard – a stark reminder of a critical business lesson, which has driven the creation of this book: the hardest part is not to become successful. It is to stay there.

Nokia's meltdown is worth studying through two lenses. On a micro level it raises questions: what actually went wrong at the company? How could a truly iconic brand widely recognised for innovation and commercial excellence turn so quickly into a stagnating organism? And more broadly Nokia's spectacular fall to earth raises a fundamental issue which is often ignored in the aftermath of a corporate collapse: what actually causes successful businesses to fail?

After all, almost every industry has its own Nokia story. The movie industry has Blockbuster. The photography industry has Kodak. Retail has Sears and Kmart. For every Apple, there is an Atari, for every Fuji a Polaroid, and for every VHS a Betamax. Story after story can be told about successful companies, which stood still or slipped back while their customers moved on without them. And the narrative is more present than ever before. For example, take a close look at the graph on page 14 showing the relationship between the development in human life span and corporate life span since the 1950s. It reveals an interesting paradox. While human beings live longer and longer, companies live shorter and shorter. In 1958 the average lifespan of a company in the S&P index, widely regarded as the best single gauge of large-cap US equities, was 61 years. Today it is 16 years. Many businesses are now dying younger, and nothing seems to indicate that corporate life expectancy will not continue to drop. Professor Richard Foster of Yale University has estimated that "by 2020, more than

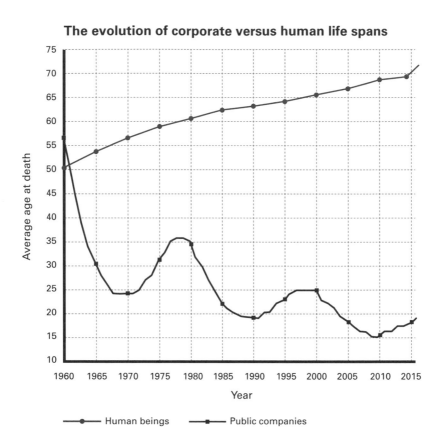

The evolution of corporate versus human life spans

The graph shows the relationship between the development in human life span (green line) and corporate life span (red line) since 1958.

three quarters of the S&P 500 will be companies that we have not yet heard of."

∗ ∗ ∗

Six months ago I delivered a lecture titled "How to create hunger in paradise" at an executive meeting in a large and very successful investment management company in London. Beforehand, the CEO sent me a list of the

10 most successful companies in his industry a decade ago compared to today. Only two companies from the first list were also on the second. His point was crystal clear: we make a big mistake if we assume that we will automatically be successful tomorrow because we are so today.

I bet that if many people reading this looked at their own industry and did the same exercise as the CEO of the investment management company they would most probably come to the same conclusion. Assuming that tomorrow will be like yesterday is a dangerous illusion.

The fall of Nokia is not just an entertaining story from a business book we skim through before putting it back on the bookshelf without further reflection. In fact, the next Nokia could be anyone. As former co-CEO of SAP, Jim Hagemann Snabe, explained to me during my research for this book: "Rapid shifts in relevance used to only happen to high-paced technology companies, but with more and more industries being impacted by the digital economy the same speed of change will hit them too. Even established industries you would never imagine being in danger are now being disrupted. No one can feel safe anymore."

Over the past five years it had been my mission to understand not only why successful companies fail at an increasingly faster rate, but also to explain how they can remain vibrant, profitable and ahead of the pack. I have spoken to CEOs from top companies, studied the research of leading psychologists, and I have reflected deeply on my own experiences as a founder and a director of organisations which have enjoyed a degree of success.

During the pages in this book I have conceptualised my findings in a format I hope you will find easy to digest. I don't like long, dry, repetitive business books of 400 pages. I like it short and sharp, and my aim is that you will finish this book on your next two-hour flight, although I sincerely hope the key messages will live on for a lot longer. They are my suggestions for how to deal with some of the toughest management questions you can imagine: how do you keep complacency out of the building when everything appears rosy? How do you act with urgency when there seems to be no obvious burning platform in sight? In other words: how do you create hunger in paradise?

The Flipside of Human Nature

Why successful companies are their own worst enemy

When companies become successful they don't just fight their competitors anymore. More than anything they fight themselves. That might sound counter-intuitive. Perhaps the statement even appears to be just another buzz-phrase invented by a fluffy business consultant, but in fact the idea is backed by 35 years of solid research by social scientists across the globe. Success produces complacency. It doesn't even have to be recent success. An organization's glory days can have ended long ago, and yet the complacency can live on, without the employees and managers being able to recognize it.

Nokia's spectacular collapse provides a textbook example. Usually the rise of the iPhone takes the centre stage when business analysts seek to explain why Nokia fell so far and fast. However, I believe the answer is simpler. Apple didn't kill Nokia. Nokia killed Nokia. The company was wounded even before the battle with Apple began. Decades of success had created a protective and complacent culture that blocked the company from reacting quickly enough to a changing landscape.

In January 2007, when Apple's charismatic owner, Steve Jobs, with his usual passion and hyper-confidence unveiled a new touchscreen smartphone called the iPhone at the Macworld convention in San Francisco, Nokia was busy celebrating success. Just a few months later the company presented an operating profit of €5.5 billion, owning 36% of the global smartphones market and selling more phones than number two and three in the industry combined. It was the culmination of a decade of total and almost intimidating dominance. A decade in which Nokia owned a market share of 60% in some countries, and accounted for a quarter of Finland's growth in GDP.

The launch of the iPhone was an indifferent parenthesis in Nokia's victory speech. As always when a competitor launched a new product, Nokia's engineers had examined the iPhone, but they quickly turned it off believing that there was nothing to worry about. They felt that it was too expensive to produce, primitive in comparison with Nokia's 3G technology, and it didn't even come close to passing Nokia's rigorous "drop test," in which a phone is dropped five feet onto concrete from a variety of angles. As Nokia CEO Olli-Pekka Kallasvuo stubbornly put it barely a year after the release of the iPhone: "From a competition perspective, iPhone is nothing but a niche product."

* * *

Olli-Pekka Kallasvuo's famous quote not only came to stand as a monument to the arrogance that took down Nokia. In a broader context it also exemplified what a large body of scientific research has proved again and again over the past four decades: success and power change the perspective through which people see the world, and often in ways that are counterproductive to sustaining success.

One of the best illustrations is the E-test, popularised by Adam Galinsky, a professor of Business at Columbia University. In his original experiment published in 2003 Galinsky asked two groups to write an essay. The first was told to write about an experience where they had felt powerful and successful. This group Galinsky called the *high power* group. The other group – which Galinsky referred to as the *low power* group – was asked to choose an experience where they had felt powerless. After having completed the essay Galinsky asked both groups to take a pen and draw a capital E on their forehead.

That task can be done in two ways: by drawing the E as though one is reading it oneself, which leads to a backward E to everyone else or so that it is legible to others, but is backward from the writer's perspective.

The outcome of Galinsky's test was thought-provoking. The *high power* group who had written an essay associating themselves with success and power were nearly three times more likely to draw a self-oriented E rather than those in the *low power* group.

Galinsky concluded that there seems to be an inverse relationship between power and the lens through which we view the world. The more powerful someone feels at a certain moment the less likely they are to comprehend how others see, think, and feel.

As with the *high power* group from Galinsky's E-experiment, success and power tend to change the perspective of companies too. A company that has built its success on a strong commitment to delight its customers and give them more than they expected can be infiltrated by bureaucracy, internal politics and power struggles. Suddenly the wrong issues dominate the agenda. Instead of focusing on how to improve customer service and increase market share, they now discuss the size of the company cars and why the chairs in the canteen are not comfortable enough. Outside-in is replaced by inside-out.

The story about SAP, the German software giant, which I will go into in more detail in another chapter, is a great example of how successful companies often get stuck with their own perspective. Year after year of huge profits created a culture in SAP where the only thing that mattered was selling as much software as possible. No one at SAP really cared about whether the customers actually used the software they bought and if it made a difference to their businesses at all. As the co-CEO Jim Hagemann Snabe explained to me when we met at SAP headquarters in Waldorf, an hour's drive outside Frankfurt: "Our attitude was arrogant. We sell you a piece of software and wish you all the best. If you have a problem, *read the bloody manual.*"

In that way success turns the company into a *selfie-*

stick organisation. Or, to borrow a line from the former General Electric's CEO Jack Welch, a company becomes a place where "everyone has their face towards the CEO and their ass toward the customer." People lose track of the market, its threats and opportunities, and – ultimately – they disconnect from what actually made them successful in the first place: "We are successful because we delight our customers" becomes "We are successful because we are SAP".

* * *

Basketball is another great example of how success can lead us into behavioural patterns that paradoxically undermine success. Of course people often think the opposite. They believe that success begets more success. But we should be careful of naturally assuming so.

For years and years in basketball players, coaches and commentators were convinced about the existence of *the hot hand* – the assumption that a player is more likely to make a successful shot if his previous shot was successful. However, most statisticians now believe that the hot hand doesn't exist. They have found that successful shots make a player shoot more, but he doesn't score more. Some studies even suggest that, paradoxically, the likelihood of subsequent baskets actually decreases because over-confidence leads the player to take shots of great difficulty.

In another study entitled *Heads I Win, Tails It's Chance*, two American psychologists, Ellen Langer and Jane Roth, asked a group of subjects to flip a coin 30 times and predict whether it would be heads up or tails up. They then told each subject how many times his or her prediction was correct, not from the factual results but from a predetermined list of results. Some were told that their predictions were mostly successful. Others were told they were average or even mostly wrong. In the final part of the study all subjects were asked to rate their general ability to predict the outcome of coin flips on a 10-point scale (0 = poor, 10 = very good).

Langer and Roth discovered that the more successful the subjects thought they were in the experiment the higher they rated their general ability to predict the outcome of the toss. Apparently, even in a discipline where success is completely random we tend to believe that our ability caused it. Feeling successful breeds what Langer and Roth call *an illusion of personal control.*

In a similar way many successful businesses are not prepared to acknowledge the role of luck in their success. When explaining their success they emphasise talent and hard work to the exclusion of chance events and external factors like for example favorable market conditions. However, false beliefs about luck are dangerous because they lead companies to assume that their success is more stable than it actually is.

* * *

I am not claiming that complacency is the only reason why successful companies fail. There are many other reasons – some of which are out of their control. A book could be written about any of those, but this one focuses on the psychological reasons, which the business literature often either neglects or is satisfied to describe in superficial terms.

At the heart of this book is the notion that success activates a set of cognitive biases that potentially prevents individuals and organizations from repeating success, something I refer to as *the flipside of human nature.* In particular three cognitive biases weigh heavily on the decisions of successful corporations.

Outcome bias: the tendency to evaluate the quality of a decision when the outcome of the decision is already known. Outcome bias is driven by the underlying assumption that good outcomes always come from good decisions and superior performance.

Escalation of commitment: when groups of people continue to rationalise their decisions, actions, and investments when faced with increasingly negative outcomes rather than alter their course. In the investment world this tendency is often described as "throwing good money after bad".

The-end-of-history illusion: this is a psychological illusion in which individuals of all ages believe they have experienced significant personal growth up to present moment, but will not substantially grow or mature in the future.

You might assume that these problems happen only

in larger institutions. But in my experience that is not necessarily the case. To a large extent it is the same cognitive biases that cause a company with 50,000 employees to fail as a company with 50. The good news is that they can be beaten. It is not an easy task though. Against the flipside of human nature even very successful companies are the underdogs.

Overriding biases means you have to act counterintuitively. When results are better than ever you need to ask increasingly sceptical questions. When you are number one you have to act as if you were number two. When there seems to be no need to change it is often the right time to drive change. This is the paradoxical nature of creating hunger in paradise. To a large extent it is about *de-biasing* your mindset and decisions by acting against what your gut instinct tells you. This book will tell you how.

Principle #1:
Never Trust Success

On a cold December evening in 2010, thousands of Newcastle United fans gathered in the streets outside St. James' Park to voice their anger at club owner Mike Ashley, who had just sacked his fifth manager in little more than three years. Inside the ground the fans vocalised their frustration at the controversial departure of manager Chris Hughton with choruses of "get out of our club", and banners describing Ashley as a "fat slug". The atmosphere that day neatly encapsulated life as a Newcastle supporter – a club that won its last domestic trophy in 1955.

Instinctively Newcastle should have all the building blocks to be successful. A billionaire businessman owner, a glorious history with 10 domestic titles, and a fan base most clubs would die for. Every other week 50,000 fervent supporters, among the highest attendance in Europe, flock to the city's football cathedral, famous for its electric and intimidating atmosphere. However, apart from a few spikes of hope in the 90s, for most of the past 60 years life as a Newcastle supporter has been filled with sadness, disillusionment and despair. As a fan describes his feelings on Talk Of The Tyne, one of the club's many online fan forums: "I define my relationship with Newcastle United as an abusive one I can't get out of. I love them dearly, we used to be such good friends, I worship them and I put them on a pedestal they often don't deserve to be on. Time and time again they let me down; they punish me, they sadden me, they anger me, they hurt me, they disappoint me, yet I keep coming back for more."

* * *

On 2 May 2012, 17 months after the controversial sacking of Chris Hughton, fortunes changed for Newcastle. With a 2-0 win away against Chelsea FC in West London, they secured a sensational fifth place finish in the Premier League. The most optimistic predictions had the team finishing mid-table, but Newcastle had exceeded everyone's expectations by breaking into the top five of the Premier League ahead of title contenders like Chelsea and Liverpool – teams that have an abundance of star players, huge budgets and trophy expectations.

With headlines like "Newcastle will be more than one season wonders" and "Newcastle have built their recent success on spirit and sweat" the newspapers hailed their achievement, and a few weeks later it came as little surprise when Alan Pardew, the manager that Ashley appointed shortly after the fan protests in December 2010, was named Premier League manager of the season.

Amid the euphoria Pardew and his coaching staff were rewarded with an extraordinary eight-year contract. That summer, Newcastle appeared on the brink of an exciting new era. Suddenly everything appeared possible again.

Yet just 11 months later Newcastle were trashed 6-0 at home to Liverpool and were facing a relegation battle with only three games left in the season. With desperation painted on his face, Pardew tried to explain the collapse in his post-match interview. "It's hard to explain what has happened. We haven't become a bad staff or a bad set of players overnight."

Many shared Pardew's confusion at Newcastle's slump. After all, this was not a temporary drop in form, where a team slips for a few games and finds footing again, but a shocking free fall. Only at the last minute Newcastle climbed clear of the relegation battle to finish 16th. Still the question lingered: how could a largely unchanged team in less than 12 months drop 11 places in the league table and earn 24 points less – one of the worst season-to-season point total drops in the history of the Premier League?

* * *

A few years ago it became clear to me that the brightest people in football don't work for the clubs. They work in the gambling industry. I am not talking about the amateur gambler who places a few bets on Saturday morning to trigger his weekly rush of adrenaline or the hope that a massive accumulator could change his life. I am talking about the pros, the guys using sophisticated mathematical models to place their bets.

When the first professional football betting syndicates started popping up in the late 90s, the bookmakers had little idea what was going on. Amid the deregulation and subsequent explosion of online betting, bookmakers started offering prices on many more different leagues around the world, but suddenly they were now competing against underground gamblers using statistical modelling and huge amounts of data to make betting decisions. These statistical models were far more accurate than the bookmakers' own probability calculations. For example, the bookmakers had no accurate idea about how good teams in the Brazilian second division were, say – or the Mexican third division. The odds they offered gamblers were more the reflection of an educated guess rather than the result of a conscious analytical process. Against the syndicates with their newly acquired statistical powers the bookmakers were fighting a losing battle.

The way a professional gambler approaches football is fascinating. His decision-making process is stripped of emotion and rooted in detailed rational analysis. The opposite is true for many football clubs. The game is overcrowded with people who have spent most of their lives in football. They have a heartfelt passion, but they have never really thought deeply about questions such as:

What key performance indicators are the most reliable to predict the future results of a team?

Which numbers can you trust in assessing team strength and which numbers mislead you?

What is the relative strength between the Swiss, the English and the German leagues?

And if a player scores 10 goals in the top flight of the

Dutch league, how many is that equivalent to in the English Premier League?

I know this is a controversial statement, but I believe that good gamblers would be able to make better decisions about transfer strategy, player assessment and squad selection than most football management teams. In fact, if professional gamblers made decisions in a way most football clubs do they would very quickly file for bankruptcy.

* * *

There is an old saying frequently used by football journalists, managers and players: the league table never lies. Professional gamblers would strongly disagree. They would argue that, actually, the league table almost always lies. This belief rises from a deep understanding of its inner mechanic. As a gambler the first commandment you must accept is that football is a game strongly influenced by randomness.

Think about it. If the outcome of a football game were only determined by skill and not luck, the best team would always win. Yet that is far from the case. Story after story can be told about teams that outplayed their opponent, but still lost.

The random nature of the game is especially emphasised in football because it is a low-scoring sport – unlike, for example, basketball and tennis. The average number of goals per game in the Premier League in recent seasons has been around 2.79, while in the NBA (the premier professional basketball league in the world) the average number of points per game is 204. As a consequence, a shot that hits the basket and bounces out is unlikely to have a big impact on the final score: in football a shot that hits the post could make all the difference between winning and losing.

Yet when clubs, coaches and fans look at the league table after 38 games they tend to believe they see a fair reflection of who were the best and the worst performing teams that season. A professional gambler understands that what you really see is a simplified story of a season constructed around a single set of summary statistics, which ignore the alternative outcomes that might have unfolded if a shot in the 87th minute hadn't been deflected in for the winning goal, or if the referee hadn't overlooked that penalty.

This is not the same as to say that successful teams are just lucky, but fortune does play a role, and sometimes a pivotal one. The low scoring nature of the game means that the best team wins less often in football than in most sports – and, ultimately, this is the reason why the league table lies. It lies less after 20 games than after ten games. And it lies less after a full season than after 20 games. However, 38 games, a full Premier League season, is still what statisticians would call a very small sample size: simply not enough games to strip out the randomness completely.

So to evaluate how well a team is performing a good gambler doesn't look at the league table. Instead he makes his decisions on the basis of underlying performance indicators which tell him much more about how a team is likely to perform in the future than its current league table position does.

* * *

While Newcastle's fall from grace remained inexplicable to Pardew, Ashley and the rest of the Newcastle board it didn't surprise the professional gamblers. They actually expected it to happen.

Take a look at the league table on page 32 showing the end of the 2011-12 Premier League season, the year Newcastle United finished fifth.

At first glance it looks like any other league table, but if we dig a layer deeper and study it through the lens of a gambler a different picture starts to emerge. Three indicators in particular convinced the professional gamblers that Newcastle United's success was unsustainable.

English Premier League Table 2011-12

Team	GP	GD	Pts
1 Manchester City	38	+64	89
2 Manchester United	38	+56	89
3 Arsenal	38	+25	70
4 Tottenham	38	+25	69
5 Newcastle	38	+5	65
6 Chelsea	38	+19	64
7 Everton	38	+10	56
8 Liverpool	38	+7	52
9 Fulham	38	−3	52
10 West Bromwich	38	−7	47
11 Swansea	38	−7	47
12 Norwich	38	−14	47
13 Sunderland	38	−1	45
14 Stoke	38	−17	45
15 Wigan	38	−20	43
16 Aston Villa	38	−16	38
17 Queens Park Rangers	38	−23	37
18 Bolton	38	−31	36
19 Blackburn	38	−30	31
20 Wolverhampton	38	−42	25

The league table after the final game of the 2011/12 Premier League season. GP = Games Played. GD = Goal Difference. Pts = Points.

Indicator 1: Goal difference

It might surprise some but goal difference – the difference between the number of goals a team scores and the number of goals it concedes – is one of the most reliable indicators of a team's strength. The diagram below shows how obvious the correlation between goal difference and points is over the last sixteen seasons of the Premier League.

Correlation between Points and Goal Difference in Premier League 2000-2016

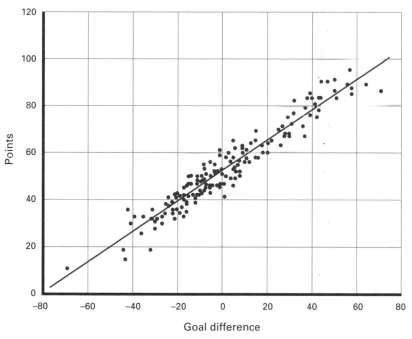

The graph shows the correlation between a team's goal difference (x-axis) and the number of points achieved (y-axis) over the last 16 Premier League seasons.

Let's now look at the final league table of the 2011-12 season again. The four teams who finished above Newcastle (Manchester City, Manchester United, Arsenal and Tottenham) were also the four teams with the best goal difference. In the same way, the four teams at the bottom

English Premier League Table 2011-12

	Team	GP	GD	Pts
1	Manchester City	38	+64	89
2	Manchester United	38	+56	89
3	Arsenal	38	+25	70
4	Tottenham	38	+25	69
5	Newcastle	38	+5	65
6	Chelsea	38	+19	64
7	Everton	38	+10	56
8	Liverpool	38	+7	52
9	Fulham	38	−3	52
10	West Bromwich	38	−7	47
11	Swansea	38	−7	47
12	Norwich	38	−14	47
13	Sunderland	38	−1	45
14	Stoke	38	−17	45
15	Wigan	38	−20	43
16	Aston Villa	38	−16	38
17	Queens Park Rangers	38	−23	37
18	Bolton	38	−31	36
19	Blackburn	38	−30	31
20	Wolverhampton	38	−42	25

The table highlights the goal difference (GD) of every team in the Premier League season 2011/12.

of the table (Queens Park Rangers, Bolton, Blackburn and Wolves) were also the four teams with the worst goal difference.

Something else about the table catches the eye: Newcastle might have 64 points, but their goal difference is only +5, a very long way behind the four top teams.

Goal Difference in the Premier League 2011-12

	Team	GP	GD	Pts
1	Manchester City	38	+64	89
2	Manchester United	38	+56	89
3	Arsenal	38	+25	70
4	Tottenham	38	+25	69
5	Newcastle	38	+5	65
6	Chelsea	38	+19	64
7	Everton	38	+10	56

From a statistical point of view, a +5 goal difference typically equates to around 55 points, which strongly indicates that Pardew and his team were extremely fortunate to end up with 10 more, on 65 points.

Indicator 2: Goal distribution

The Premier League season is a culmination of 760 games, about 8,800 shots and 1,000 goals. But not all goals are equally important. The third goal in a 3-0 win is obviously not as important as the winning goal in a 3-2 win.

While the number of goals teams score and concede over a season tends to be a solid reflection of their true strength, how effectively their goals are distributed is to a large extent driven by randomness. In an extreme case, everything else being equal, a goal difference of 0 over seven games could leave a team with two very different outcomes.

0-1, 0-1, 0-1, 6-0, 0-1, 0-1, 0-1 (3 points out of 21)

1-0, 1-0, 1-0, 0-6, 1-0, 1-0, 1-0 (18 points out of 21)

Not surprisingly, Newcastle's 2011-12 season was driven by an extremely effective goal distribution. A breakdown of the 65 points the team achieved shows eight wins with one goal, nine wins with two goals and three major defeats of 2-5, 0-5 and 0-4. In the mind of a gambler such a goal distribution clearly indicates that a team is getting more points than its underlying performance justifies.

Indicator 3: Shot differential

It is statistically well documented that the best football teams over time produce more shots on goal than their opponents. A key stat to measure the quality of a team's performance is therefore what gamblers call *shot differential* (defined as the difference between the number of shots on goal a team produces and the number of shots their opponent produces).

Looking at the shot differential of the top six teams in the 2011-12 Premier League season it becomes even clearer that Newcastle's successive run was unsustainable.

Shot differential in the Premier League 2011/12

Team	Home	Away	Total
1 Manchester City	+12.3	+5.3	+8.8
2 Manchester United	+8.5	−1.2	+3.6
3 Arsenal	+9.5	+3.1	+6.3
4 Tottenham	+10.4	+2.1	+6.2
5 Newcastle	+3.5	−6.3	−1.4
6 Chelsea	+8.8	+2.8	+5.8

The table shows the shot differential of the top six teams in the 2011/12 Premier League season when playing at home, away and in total. Data source: 21st Club (www.21stclub.com).

Newcastle secured fifth place with a total shot differential of -1.4. On average that season their opponents had 1.4 shots more on goal per game, which meant that Newcastle had the sixth worst shot differential of the league.

When a good gambler spots a team with a positive goal difference driven by a negative shot differential, it sets alarm bells ringing. It can almost only be caused by unsustainable high conversion rates (the percentage of a team or a player's shots converted to goals). In Newcastle's case this is best illustrated by the Senegalese striker Papiss Cisse, whose 13 goals in 14 games was a key reason for Newcastle's high finish. More interestingly, Cisse's 13 goals were driven by a spectacular 33% conversion rate. In comparison Lionel Messi, the world's best player, converted 20% of his shots to goals that same season.

Even for the world's best strikers, conversion rates above 25% are almost impossible to sustain season after season. Having conversion rates at about 30% in football is like a publicly traded company having a really high share price, while at the same time also having really low customer satisfaction. It is possible for one year, but impossible to maintain over time.

The professional gamblers were never in doubt: Newcastle's fifth place was one of the biggest overachievements in the history of the Premier League – a fragile bubble that could burst any time.

* * *

Let's revisit the question from the start of the chapter: how can a largely unchanged team drop 11 places in the league table and earn 24 points less in the space of a season?

Well, Pardew was probably spot on with his analysis when he admitted that "we haven't become a bad staff or a bad set of players overnight." Newcastle had not become a worse football team. They had just become less lucky.

The black line in the following graph shows the number of points Newcastle achieved in the 2011-12 season, when they finished 5th, and 2012-13 season, when they finished 16th. The red line shows the number of *expected points*, a term gamblers use to describe the underlying true performance level.

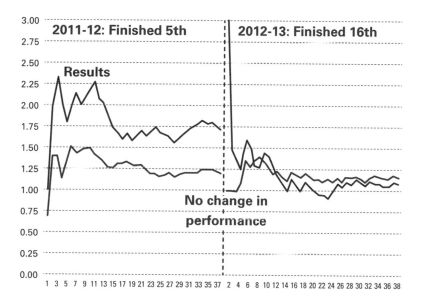

The black line of the graph shows the number of points Newcastle achieved in the 2011/12 and 2012/13 Premier League seasons. The red line of the graph shows their number of expected points throughout the two seasons. Expected points is a term used to explain the number of points a team was expected to achieve based on its underlying performance level. Data source: 21st Club (www.21stclub.com).

The graph shows an almost unchanged performance level (the red line) throughout both seasons. The drop off in results was not caused by worse performance, but simply by random variation. Or as the professional gamblers would put it: Newcastle's results had regressed to the mean – that is, having enjoyed a period of extremely good luck their fortune reverted to normal.

This insight reframes our original question. Now the key question becomes: why did Newcastle's board not see this inevitable downturn coming? How could they allow themselves to rest in the belief that they were successful when the underlying performance indicators clearly showed it was not that simple? Was it lack of insight? Pure incompetence? Or did Newcastle simply not want the music to stop?

I believe Newcastle was blinded by one of the most common management delusions: OUTCOME BIAS, the assumption that good results are always the consequence of good decisions. Or, to put it another way: success turns luck into genius.

* * *

In 1975 the American management professor Barry Staw conducted a thought-provoking demonstration of how outcome bias impacts people's decision-making.

In his famous experiment, Staw asked groups of participants to estimate a company's future sales and earnings per share based on a set of financial data. Afterwards, he told some groups they had performed well, and others that they had performed poorly. Staw did this completely randomly, without assessing the actual performance of the groups. He then asked the participants to rate how well their groups had collaborated in the process of solving the task.

Interestingly, it turned out that the groups who were

told they had performed consistently well described their collaboration as having been highly cohesive, with great communication, and superior motivation.

On the other hand, those groups who were told they had performed poorly described their collaboration in much more downbeat terms. Staw concluded that whatever we know about the outcome strongly affects how we evaluate the quality of the process.

* * *

The story of Newcastle's 2011-12 season is a prime example of outcome bias. Their fifth-place finish left the world of football not only full of admiration but with a need to explain the success. Among the most common explanations were the club's courage in giving young, hungry players the opportunity to play; its ability to find diamonds in the rough like Cisse, and Pardew's attractive style of football.

When the same team dropped to 16th the following season the story reversed completely. Now Newcastle had too many young players, the transfer policy had failed and the team lacked enough experienced English players who knew what the league was about. Suddenly the attractive style of play was naive and lacked defensive awareness. The same characteristics that were supposedly the reason for their success were now the reason for their failure.

As the social psychologist Elliot Aronson has identified, we are not rational beings: we are rationalising beings. Our brains are story-making mechanisms wired to detect patterns, no matter whether they really exist or not. When a team, business or person does something unexpected we immediately start searching for a story that justifies it and makes sense to us. We may not know exactly why something happened, but we want to feel we know it.

The idea that the decline of Newcastle was primarily caused by random variation is almost impossible for some people to accept. We want the comfort of a plausible explanation, and randomness is not a comfortable option. Therefore we look at the league table and build a narrative that fits.

This natural tendency to let the outcome dictate the story about the underlying performance is one of the biggest threats to successful organisations. And when navigating in a reality where actions and outcomes are imperfectly linked, there is only one way to fight back: attack your success with the same level of scepticism as your failures.

* * *

Jorgen Vig Knudstorp is sitting in a white shirt and a pair of light trousers, with his characteristic calm, thoughtful personality, at his humble office at the Lego headquarters in Billund, a small town with 6,000 inhabitants in western Denmark.

"A good friend of mine, who is a consultant, often challenges me by saying that when he walks into Lego today, he sees the same thing that he saw when he walked into Nokia in 2007," he says, smiling.

The CEO of the Lego Group sits for a little while without saying anything before he continues.

"He is right. In reality, no companies are more than a few years from failure. It is important to remember, and it's something I try to remind my organisation of again and again."

Two months before our meeting Knudstorp had presented another record result: 25% growth, the fifth consecutive year with more than 20% growth and ten consecutive years of record profits. All delivered in a stagnating market. Recently Lego even surpassed Ferrari and Red Bull at the top of the highly respected Brand Finance list of the world's most powerful brands.

The success of the Danish toy company is truly impressive, and that is exactly what worries Knudstorp. Because how do you stay humble when a company cashes in more than a billion dollars in profits every year? How do you keep respecting your competitors, when you are more profitable than your three closest rivals combined? And how do you get more than 10,000 employees, who perceive themselves as very successful, to understand that good results are not necessarily the consequence of their good decisions?

* * *

The first time I met Knudstorp was almost 10 years ago. Back then he was only 34 years old yet, as the newly appointed CEO of Lego, he had just managed to save the company from a looming bankruptcy. Today Knudstorp has different challenges, but, as he notes, it hasn't necessarily made the job easier. Knudstorp believes that in many ways it is tougher to manage a successful business than a company in crisis.

Why? Well, in a crisis people are forced to ask questions about everything they do. They understand why it is important to walk an extra mile, because the premise is clear: improve – or you are going out of business.

In times of success it is different. Suddenly there is no obvious burning need to drive improvement. No one really questions the success because the results obviously speak for themselves – and it becomes almost impossible for people to imagine a reality without this success.

This is the reason why Knudstorp is obsessed with creating a culture where people do not get shot down when they challenge Lego's success internally. In fact, he tries to create a culture that celebrates what he calls "the complainers". On his internal blog Knudstorp thanks and praises those who criticise him or the organization. His belief is that if you take the time to formulate a critique of your own organization and share it publicly, it's because you're passionate about it and sincerely concerned about how the organization is performing. As he puts it: "I wouldn't say that I provide diplomatic immunity to complainers, but I make sure that the employees who are asking the uncomfortable questions and taking a critical position towards Lego don't get purged."

According to Knudstorp, history is packed with examples of humans blindly assuming that because they were successful yesterday, they will probably also be successful tomorrow. He believes one of his most crucial leadership tasks is to tear down that illusion by making employees reflect on the actual reason for their success. When a company fails it is natural to dig for the reasons – why did we fail and how can we get better? But when a company is successful it often just cruises on, expecting the success to continue automatically. Its leaders don't stop for a moment and ask themselves: why did we actually succeed? Does it come down to a set of unique market conditions? Was it just pure luck? Or did we actually truly outperform our competitors?

When navigating in a noisy environment strongly influenced by political regulations, macroeconomics and sometimes even pure randomness, it is easy to confuse sound leadership with good market conditions. As Knudstorp emphasised to me: "Every successful company should carefully consider strategically as well as philosophically what creates its success. For example, at the moment a number of macroeconomic and structural factors give Lego a temporary advantage. Last week I stood up in front of 200 of our managers at a conference and said: You are doing a great job, but you also need to be aware that a number of circumstances you have no control over give you 20-30% tailwind on the bike path, and no one knows how long that will last."

* * *

When Knudstorp spots symptoms of complacency in Lego he starts touring the organisation with his favourite story to remind people that their success may not be as solid as they think. He'll tell them about a police station that Lego made 10,000 sets of a few years back, and sent into the stores, only to discover that there had been an error during the packing process. One little grey building block was missing, and without it, it was impossible to build the police station.

Despite the fact that Lego's customer service replaces everything for free if consumers believe that they have lost items or something is missing, they only heard from less than two percent of the people who had bought the police station with the missing piece. In other words, 98 out of 100 consumers who bought the set, opened it and had an unsatisfactory experience, yet they never complained.

A complaint rate of two percent in the toy industry is not a disaster. Lego could easily just have cruised on without really noticing the few complaining consumers. However, to Knudstorp the police station became the perfect illustration of one of his anti-complacency messages: you can't judge success on face value. Just because only 1-2% of people complain does not necessarily mean that you are successful. Often they only represent a much larger, 'hidden' proportion of consumers.

As Knudstorp explained to me: "We had a failure rate at 100% on the product, but we heard from less than two percent. It's really worth noticing, because that might mean that when we hear from 5,000 dissatisfied consumers, they might actually represent 1,000,000 dissatisfied consumers."

* * *

Lego has mastered the art of deliberately questioning success. I found one of the best examples of this mentality in the company's consumer service department located in Slough, 40 minutes outside central London. From here, Lego's team helps consumers in 16 different languages with questions about everything from how to build a tricky model to how to get a missing brick if your dog has eaten the one you needed.

The consumer service team is behind one of the most impressive numbers in Lego, their extremely high Net Promoter Score (NPS) – a measure of how many of your customers would actively recommend your product or service to others. After each call to Lego's consumer service the customer is asked to rate on a scale from 1-10 the extent to which, based on their experience, they would recommend Lego to their friends and family?

More than 9 out of 10 reply that they will actively recommend Lego. In the retail industry that is simply in a league of its own: most retail brands are more than happy with a recommendation rate of 65%.

However, it has become clear to Lego's consumer service team that the impressive NPS score doesn't reflect the entire truth. When Lego ask independent firms, with their 'mystery shoppers', to call its consumer service acting as a customer and rate their experience, barely five out of 10 would actively recommend it. The same is true when internal staff at Lego, as a part of the company's quality control, re-listen to the recorded calls between customers and Lego's consumer service and afterwards rate the performance. Again, the rating is significantly lower than those of Lego's consumers. So what is the reason? Why do Lego's consumers believe that Lego does a better job than Lego do themselves? Just because the answer is unclear, it doesn't mean that Lego will not keep trying to answer the question.

* * *

In football, the league table often lies, and the same is true for a customer satisfaction score like NPS. The phenomenon driving this is the so-called 'Halo Effect'. In simple terms this means that customers often buy product A made by company X, not because of the attributes or benefits of the product, but because they had a favorable experience with product B, another product made by company X.

A classic example is how the success of the iPod in the mid-2000s had a direct impact on the sales of Apple Mac laptops. Because consumers fell in love with the iPod they were automatically likely to purchase other Apple products, which they otherwise wouldn't have considered. That's how the Halo effect works: if we see a brand in a positive light, it is difficult subsequently to darken that light. Similarly, studies have shown how good-looking people are automatically rated as intelligent and successful too: one trait of a person or brand is used to make an overall judgment.

Lego's unparalleled success and popularity have spread its 'Halo' all over its interactions with customers, and ultimately this is what makes the NPS score look better than the underlying performance actually justifies.

As Lego's Senior Director of Consumer Services, Sophie Patrikios, explained to me: "We tend to believe that when we have good results, it is because we made all the right decisions, but there is often more to the story. We constantly try to remind ourselves that good results are not necessarily a product of good decisions."

Wise managers like Patrikios resist the natural tendency to make attributions based solely on outcomes. Instead they go out of their way to find independent evidence for good performance, such as using mystery shoppers. This is the reason why Patrikios doesn't trust Lego's NPS score. To her the more interesting question is: If our consumers didn't feel any goodwill towards the Lego brand, how would they rate their experience? If an unknown company delivered the same level of service that Lego does, how impressed would consumers then be?

* * *

What makes Lego determined to strive to surpass their own records is the same mindset that makes a professional gambler repeatedly outperform the market: the willingness to continuously fight the influence of *outcome bias* on their decisions.

Our brains are hard-wired to want a narrative that clearly explains why the deserving succeeded while the arrogant failed, but good gamblers and management teams understand that the reality is more complex. They understand that just because events and outcomes appear linked this does not mean that they necessarily are. Bad outcomes are not always the consequence of bad performances; and good outcomes don't always mean someone acted brilliantly.

Think about it. If Newcastle's board had fully understood and accepted the interference of outcome bias, would they have rewarded their manager with an eight-year contract? Would they really have believed that this was the beginning of a new era? And would they have entered the next season without significant investment in improving the team?

Ashley and his board clearly did not undergo the rigorous self-analysis that organisations like Lego practice, with outcomes separated from inputs. It is demanding, especially in times of success. Very few companies are prepared to accept that good results are not necessarily a consequence of their brilliant strategy. It simply requires an extra mental gear to judge actions on their merits rather than simply building a narrative that fits once we know the outcome, but this is the only way to override *outcome bias*. To stay successful year after year, decade after decade, in a reality where *"the league table often lies"* companies must treat their successes with the same scepticism as their failures. After all, luck might help you reach the top, but it won't help you stay there.

Principle #2:
If It Ain't broke,
Consider Breaking it

Every time Jim Hagemann Snabe watches *Butch Cassidy and the Sundance Kid* it reminds him why successful companies perish. His favourite scene is the one where the film's anti-heroes are being hunted by various cops after a string of train robberies and end up trapped at the edge of a cliff. Despite several failed attempts to reform their lives and go straight, the two notorious outlaws now find themselves in a situation with only two options remaining: surrender and accept a death sentence or jump from the cliff into the raging river 100 feet below and pray for a miracle.

To Hagemann Snabe the scene is thought-provoking, because the fall of successful companies follows a similar chronology. Leaders ignore the early indicators that something is wrong, hesitate to drive change while they can, and one day they find themselves at the edge of the cliff with only two options: file for bankruptcy or risk the jump from the cliff.

It was in the early months of 2010 that Hagemann Snabe started to realise that the company he led at the time, the German software giant SAP, would soon start to veer towards the edge of the cliff if they didn't react.

Hagemann Snabe and his colleague Bill McDermott, an American sales executive, had only just been appointed co-CEOs of SAP, a company founded in 1972 by five visionary German engineers who believed that business software would become the next big thing and therefore decided to break out of IBM to pursue their dream. During the first 38 years of its existence the company established a heavy dominance in the market for ERP (enterprise resource planning) systems, and became a well-oiled profit machine with a customer list that most businesses would die for. As Hagemann Snabe confidently stated to me: "Mention the 100 companies you admire the most, and I will guarantee you that at least 80 of them are customers of SAP."

SAP appeared to have escaped the 2008 financial crisis with only small scratches, and looking far less battered than most of its competitors. And when Hagemann Snabe and McDermott reported their first key financial figures to the market a few months after their appointment in February 2010, analysts and investors greeted the message with the usual applause. With a 16% global market share, 27.5% profit margin and impressive customer loyalty SAP had, once again, emphasised its status as a true rock star of the stock market.

However, beneath the polished surface a worrying

picture was emerging. The success appeared to be more fragile than the headline figures suggested. Hagemann Snabe and McDermott knew it. While the stock market celebrated SAP, the two co-CEOs had growing concerns that if the company continued on its course it would eventually end up next to Butch Cassidy and the Sundance Kid at the edge of the cliff. Instead of waiting until forced to change by the market, Hagemann Snabe and McDermott decided to initiate radical change themselves, setting out to re-invent SAP from a position of strength.

* * *

Companies can measure their success by looking at two kinds of performance indicators: *lagging* and *leading*. While *lagging* indicators measure the quality of past performance, *leading* indicators are predictive, painting a picture of how you are likely to perform in the future if you continue on your current course.

Imagine, for example, someone is trying to lose weight and they want to monitor their progress. They can do that by simply measuring their weight. Or they can measure their daily intake of calories and/or the number of calories burned per day. While your weight (a *lagging* indicator) summarises how well you've done up until now, your daily calorie intake and calorie burn (*leading* indicators) indicate how successful you will be in the future.

Successful companies are typically very good at measuring *lagging* performance indicators, for example revenue, profit margin, ROI and costs. However, they also tend to be poor at measuring *leading* indicators, such as contracts under negotiation, speed of innovation and customer satisfaction. This creates an obvious problem: *lagging indicators* can paint a picture of an organisation in great shape, whilst *leading indicators* can reveal dark clouds on the horizon. The lack of attention to *leading indicators* potentially creates a false sense of stability, like a doctor who every year measures the height and weight of a patient with bad drinking and smoking habits without checking his blood pressure or heart rate. Superficially the patient looks healthy, but because of his current lifestyle he may still have long-term health problems that are yet to reveal themselves.

This is a key reason why successful companies hesitate to change before it is too late. In organisations, the disease of complacency doesn't develop quickly like an allergic reaction to eating a bag of peanuts. It develops like a lifestyle disease where the delay between cause (establishing unhealthy eating habits) and effect (diabetes, heart diseases, some cancers) takes a lot longer, often decades. And for that reason, successful companies can get away with adopting bad habits without feeling an urgent need to change behaviour.

Small opportunities are being missed, new and unconventional competitors are being ignored and critical questions are not being asked. But no one notices the gradually changing environment, because the balance sheet is still healthy. Then one day it all falls apart. At the time it may feel like an enormous and unpredictable shock, but most likely the rot started a long time ago with ignorance and slowly slipping standards. This is the principle of gradualism. Incremental changes over a sufficient period of time tend to go unnoticed, in particular when companies use the wrong performance metric.

* * *

In the mid-2000s, Starbucks almost went out of business because the company failed to diagnose its long-term health issues. The management team had become obsessed with the company's stock price – and particularly how many new stores opened during a quarter – so that it completely overlooked that many customers who used to come in twice a day had for some reason stopped going in for their afternoon treats. As the chairman of the company, Howard Schultz, explained in his book *Onward:* "The damage was slow and quiet, incremental, like a single loose thread that unravels a sweater inch by inch." When the problem became obvious and the stock price dropped 42% in one year it was almost too late to save the company. Starbucks was losing $6 million per day.

In a last-ditch attempt to stave off failure, Schultz and his team decided to give Starbucks a radical makeover, replacing all of its espresso machines with more sophisticated models, rolling out a new design for all stores, and reorganising its supply chain to get products to stores more efficiently. They even closed their 7,100 U.S. stores for 3½ hours to retrain their baristas in the art of making the perfect espresso.

Starbucks managed to alter its course just before arriving at the edge of the cliff, but not all companies act while there is still time. Instead they end up at the corporate graveyard, reminding us all that the battle against complacency starts with the willingness to confront the underlying need for change before it is visible, not waiting until it becomes blindingly obvious.

* * *

Back to SAP, where to Hagemann Snabe and McDermott in 2010 the writing on the wall was clear. SAP's success formula was about to expire. The *lagging* performance indicators showed a company in control of its own destiny, but this was just paper over the cracks. Underneath, the *leading* indicators gave rise to serious concerns. Four patterns in particular convinced the co-CEOs that radical changes had to happen:

Pattern 1:
Lagging: High sales figures
Leading: Low adoption rates

Software is sold on the promise of what it can do for a company. However, in reality many customers struggle to implement it properly, and as a consequence, a software company can have great sales figures but, if adoption is poor, not offer real value to its customers. The company may seem successful, but really it is just leaving customers with unused software licenses on the shelf, which will inevitably lead to declining sales figures in the future.

The discussion about sales vs. impact was absent at SAP. No one in the company had any real insight into how actively customers used the software they bought. And even more concerning, no one really cared. To confront the problem, Hagemann Snabe and McDermott requested data collection on SAP software adoption rates, and the reality hit SAP hard. Despite brilliant sales figures, in some cases less than 15% of the employees at SAP's customers were active users of the SAP software they had bought.

SAP had trapped itself in a vicious cycle, one that celebrated the velocity of sales instead of the difference the company made to its customers. To Hagemann Snabe and McDermott the low adoption rates constituted a massive risk. If another company were to enter the market with software solutions that were easier to implement, SAP wouldn't be able to bounce back. It was a ticking time bomb.

Pattern 2
Lagging: Growing revenue
Leading: Negative growth in new business

SAP's dominance of the enterprise resource planning market was founded on an extremely profitable business model. First, SAP sold its customers ERP management software for a significant lump sum. Then it invoiced its customers a maintenance fee of around a fifth of the original purchase every year to cover support, corrections and future updates. Of SAP's yearly revenue of 11 billion euros in 2010, around 50% came from maintenance fees. As Alex Atzberger, Head of Strategy in SAP, tellingly put it to me: "This is a beautiful business model when you have 100,000 customers."

However, the risk of such a beautiful business model is that it masks the company's real performance. Between five and six billion euros of maintenance fees rolling into the bank account every year didn't reflect how SAP was performing or how well the company was driving innovation. It was a *lagging* indicator explaining how SAP had done five, ten, or even 15 years ago when the customers first acquired the software. A much more solid indication of SAP's current performance came by looking at the growth in sales of new software – and in 2010 the trend was negative.

More than anything SAP looked like a company trying to squeeze the last drop of money out of its historic success, and profoundly struggling to find new growth in the market.

Pattern 3:

Lagging: High customer loyalty

Leading: Low customer satisfaction

Historically, SAP's customer loyalty had been in a league of its own, and that was still the case in 2010. But nevertheless a dangerous trend was starting to emerge.

At the peak of the global financial crisis in 2009 SAP's executive team made a decision they would later regret. They sent a letter to all customers to inform them that their maintenance fees would be increasing from 17% to 22%. Whereas the price rise looked like a no-brainer to SAP, because it was in line with the price point of competing products and would improve their bottom line with 500 million euros immediately, it caused deep discontent in the customer base. Still battered by the financial crisis in 2008 and 2009, most customers already felt they were paying too much for software, and increasing the maintenance fees still further without delivering new value came across as evidence of SAP's arrogance.

An ERP system is absolutely *mission critical* to a company, because it automates many back office functions related to technology, services and human resources. That also means that switching to a new ERP system involves both big risks and high costs, and as consequence customers felt trapped in SAP's business model. The relationship was starting to look like a failing marriage where customers no longer stayed with SAP because they loved them, but because they couldn't get rid of them. As a consequence, customer satisfaction went into freefall in 2010.

Pattern 4:
Lagging: Still outperforming conventional competitors
Leading: Threatened by unconventional competitors

Hagemann Snabe has a theory that any technology-driven industry sees a radical change roughly every ten years. In between, lots of buzzwords pop up, but only once every tenth year does one of those actually create a significant innovation. And, at that point, everything changes. The competitive landscape fragments, and the players are no longer the same.

When Hagemann Snabe and McDermott took charge of SAP in 2010 they picked up early signals that buzzwords like mobile, cloud and data analytics had substance to them. Customers had started to opt out of the heavy CRM systems and preferred more flexible and cheaper cloud solutions. What's more, it was no longer *the usual suspects* like Oracle and Microsoft who were challenging SAP.

In just a few years, new and unconventional competitors like Salesforce.com and SuccessFactors, who previously had not been on SAP's radar, had emerged to become multimillion-dollar businesses with very aggressive growth rates. They were marching into the offices of SAP's customers proclaiming that SAP software belonged in the past. And customers seemed to agree. They perceived SAP as a slow and bureaucratic company to do business with, not as a company they would speak to about all the new exciting stuff like big data, mobile and cloud. SAP was clearly starting to lose relevance.

* * *

Hagemann Snabe and McDermott grasped that SAP's success was unsustainable – and that travelling down the same well-worn path would lead to a situation where SAP was no longer the preferred strategic business solution for companies. Yet the biggest challenge for successful companies is not to identify the problem, or even rationally understand the need for change. It is to make an emotional decision to say goodbye to the past and drive radical change even though the headline figures seem to be in good shape.

Nokia, for instance, was fully aware of the rise of touchscreen phones. The company even produced its own touchscreen prototype seven years before Apple launched its first iPhone. As the Nokia CEO Jorma Ollila said in an interview in 2000: "There is a big paradigm shift coming. In ten years' time, I would like Nokia to be dubbed as the company that brought mobility and the Internet together." But still, despite understanding where the market was going, Nokia had so much emotional capital invested in the recipe that made them so successful that they didn't adapt until it was too late.

Digital photography didn't come out of the blue either. Kodak saw it coming. In fact it was a Kodak employee who originally invented the technology behind digital photography in 1975, but his bosses never let it see the light of day and paid the price.

As these examples prove, the transition from one business model to the next doesn't happen overnight. Even when it comes to truly remarkable and game-changing innovations, successful companies are often entirely aware of what is happening around them. They have plenty of time to reach and adapt, yet still end up hesitating for too long, finding themselves paralysed by what psychologists call an *escalation of commitment to a failing course*; a pattern of behaviour in which humans continue to rationalise their decisions and actions when faced with increasingly negative outcomes rather than alter their course.

On the first day of Professor Max Bazerman's MBA negotiation course at Harvard Business School, he introduces his students to his famous $20 dollar auction. Bazerman announces the game by waving a $20 bill in the air, and offers it up for auction. Everyone can bid for it, but there are two rules. The first is that bids are to be made in one-dollar increments. The second is a bit more complex. Whereas the winner of the auction gets the money, the runner-up must honour his/her last bid yet receives nothing in return. In other words, Bazerman creates a scenario in which the person at number two ends up as the auction's biggest loser.

The auction always starts out fast and furious. Many are motivated by the opportunity to win $20 on the cheap, and the bids fly until the auction reaches the $12 to $16 range. At that point it becomes clear to the MBA students that the competition is fierce, and one by one they begin to pull out. Eventually all but the two highest bidders have dropped out, and they soon realise that they are locked in. Say the two highest bidders have bids of $16 and $17. The $16 bidder has a choice to make: bid $18 or suffer a $16 loss.

It is exactly at this moment that the psychology of the auction changes. Up to this point the students were driven to earn some quick and easy cash. Now the fear of losing sets in, and people stop playing to win and start trying to avoid losing. From a rational perspective the right decision is to accept a loss and stop the auction before it runs off the rails, but it is easier said than done.

The last two MBA students are fighting tooth and nail to avoid incurring the loss, and their bids keep rising. Of course, at the moment when the auction passes 20 dollars the class breaks into massive cheers and laughter. But it does not stop there. The fear of the looming loss continues to push up the price. 21, 22, 23, 50, $100... the record in Professor Bazerman's classes is $204.

In all the years Bazerman has run the experiment, he has never lost a single dollar. Whether it is students or experienced executives who participate in the auction, the pattern is the same. When the two highest bidders in the auction are locked in, one of the strongest mechanisms in the human psyche kicks in, our tendency to stick with a strategy that we have committed to, even though it is obviously wrong.

* * *

The $20 auction provides an excellent demonstration of how *escalation of commitment to a failing course* often drives organisations into denial and prevents them from changing before it is too late. To make my point further, take a look at the following three quotes by Blockbuster CEO Jim Keyes in the two years before the company filed for bankruptcy in 2010.

2008: CEO Jim Keyes expresses doubt about Netflix in an interview:

"I've been frankly confused by the fascination that everybody has with Netflix... Netflix doesn't really have or do anything that we can't or don't already do ourselves."

And a few months later:

"Netflix is not even on the radar screen in terms of competition."

May 2010, in an interview with Fast Company, Jim Keyes is asked whether Blockbuster's financial troubles are due in part to Netflix's success.

"No, I don't know where that comes from"

In less than three years, Netflix stock rose by 500%, while during the same period Blockbuster stock declined by 90%. The threat of Netflix was obvious to everyone, including Blockbuster, yet its management team insisted it was business as usual.

The more successful a person or company has been with a plan or strategy the more difficult it is to change course. Blockbuster had lots of super-smart people with expensive MBA educations – a course where the first thing you learn is the sunk cost fallacy: that money and effort invested in the past shouldn't influence what is the right decision in the future. But saying goodbye to yesterday is easier said than done.

Nokia's failure provides another example. The accelerating success of iPhone in late 2007 and early 2008 started an avalanche of rationalisation in Nokia. Initially, it was mostly about the fact that there was a camera in the iPhone that barely worked. Technically, the phone was mediocre based on many parameters: it failed colossally on the drop tests, and the battery time was a joke. Nokia's engineers even produced a number of benchmark documents that clearly showed how its phones were superior to the iPhone on almost all parameters.

These arguments eased the tension internally for a while, but as the iPhone's sales numbers doubled from 2008 to 2009, further panic spread in Nokia. Yet still some in the company pointed to the high price of the iPhone, reducing the numbers who could afford it, or were willing to pay for it. There were many in Nokia who also believed that when the hype died down, the iPhone would become just another niche product.

As one Nokia manager told me: "We behaved as the band that played on the Titanic. We just stood there and continued to smile, play and keep the party going, even though the water was pouring in, and the ship sinking deeper and deeper."

* * *

In 2010 SAP could have become a sinking ship too, and the internal dialogue had started to sound eerily similar to the conversations at Nokia and Blockbuster a few years before they went under. As Hagemann Snabe explained to me: "People were aware that there were challenges, but not enough to justify radical changes. After all, most companies would rave about a 28% profit margin. Yes, the sales of new software were declining, but hey, that's just the last repercussions of the financial crisis. Everyone feels them. And yes, some customers have started to become unhappy and have left, but they will come back when they realize that they need us."

The vast majority of employees as well as managers at SAP seemed ignorant of the fact that the company was potentially only a few years' away from becoming irrelevant. Their attitude was that if they just closed their eyes and kept doing business as usual – only just a bit more efficiently – their problems would pass.

To save SAP, Hagemann Snabe and McDermott had to find a way to stop the *emotional commitment to the failing course* and instead drive people to change before it was too late. In their view, the core of the problem was how SAP staff perceived themselves and the company's relationship to its customers. SAP had been successful for such a long time that their workforce had built an almost unbreakable emotional attachment to what seemed to be the obvious vehicle driving the success: the ERP software system.

"When we asked the employees what they thought SAP was, their response was: 'We are the world's largest ERP system distributor,'" McDermott explained to me on the phone from the company's North American headquarters in Philadelphia.

To the co-CEOs this was a crucial misconception. SAP was a lot more than just that. The core purpose of SAP was not just to be an ERP system distributor but rather to help companies manage their resources more effectively. The ERP software system was just the vehicle for that to happen.

However, as long as people at SAP had all their emotional capital invested in being an ERP system provider they would not be prepared to drive the changes necessary to reinvent the company and find new growth opportunities.

To break the pattern Hagemann Snabe and McDermott had to give people at SAP a strong reason to change. They had to rediscover who they really were and imagine who they could be, and the first step was to break the internal perception of SAP being simply an ERP system provider.

* * *

One of the most famous gigs in rock'n'roll history is the Beatles playing Shea Stadium in front of 56,000 screaming fans in 1965, setting a new world record for a concert in terms of attendance and gross revenue.

The concert came to stand as the height of Beatle mania in the 60s, but as Paul McCartney later revealed the concert also symbolized the beginning of the end for the band, who broke up four years later. "At the Shea Stadium the crowd was so loud that we could no longer hear ourselves when we played," he said.

The incomparable success of the Beatles drove them to play mega concerts for bigger and bigger crowds, but amidst the mass euphoria and hysteria the band stopped hearing their own music.

Like the Beatles, many successful companies also reach a point where they stop hearing their own music. The story tends to follow a certain chronology: a company starts out with the purpose of solving X problem. Things take off. Word gets out. Demand increases and boosts the profit. The brand goes on autopilot. Everybody assumes success will continue, and gradually the memory of why the company was started in the first place becomes fuzzy. Then one day someone comes along with a better solution to X problem, but rather than fighting the threat with innovation, the company desperately hangs onto old solutions as if it was entitled to perpetual success.

This is what happened to the publishing industry. Year after year publishers sold so many books that they assumed they were in the book industry. But such a view is too narrow. In reality publishers are in the business of telling stories that engage people, and the book is just one of many vehicles to deliver it. The success of the printed book over several decades led publishers to forget what they really were, and so many of them missed out on technological developments, which had a huge impact on their industry.

Kodak, too, fell into the same trap: identifying its market in product terms, not benefit terms. The success of the analogue camera made Kodak believe that that its market was photographic film, and as a consequence it became obsessed with selling customers cheap cameras and relying on them to buy lots of expensive film. But Kodak's real market was not photographic film, it was *capturing memories*, and because the company never really grasped this concept it failed to stay relevant in a market switching from film to digital. The phone camera arrived and ate Kodak's lunch.

* * *

Reinvention has become a buzzword but too often it is used without an understanding its true meaning. What it really means in business terms is *strategic change that reinforces the company's purpose*. Take Netflix as an example. The small start-up from California began taking on Blockbuster by introducing a business model that used DVD delivery by mail. But more interestingly, when Netflix became successful it set out to reinvent itself by capturing the technology that would replace physical copies of films – digital streaming over the internet. Netflix implemented streaming long before customers began to demand it, and reaped the rewards.

While Blockbuster desperately tried to defend its thousands of stores as if they were protected species, Netflix understood that it was not in the business of sending out DVDs in the mail. It was in the business of distributing entertainment, and in the future customers would want this service delivered online, available with just one push on the remote control.

This is an absolute key lesson in what keeps successful companies successful. A company is not just the physical manifestation of how it makes money. It is something more and deeper than that. Investing your emotional shares in who you really are, your psychological heartbeat, rather than into what you are making is what allows you to adapt to a changing business landscape before it is too late.

* * *

So how was SAP able to change course away from the path leading towards the edge of the cliff? For more than a decade the company's ERP systems had gone from strength to strength in boardrooms across the world, but the business model was running out of steam. SAP had to start hearing its own music again, and to Hagemann Snabe and McDermott that meant realising that the company wasn't just about ERP systems. In its deepest essence, SAP is about helping companies become successful by managing their resources more effectively. And whereas the market for ERP systems was in decline, the market for helping companies manage their resources was as big as ever.

Framing its identify this way not only allowed SAP to detach itself from the emotional attachment to being an ERP system company. It also made the company see its potential with fresh eyes. As Hagemann Snabe, who has now stepped down from his position to become part of the firm's supervisory board, explained to me: "We started to think: 'What if we in addition to helping companies manage traditional resources like money, materials and people could also help them manage scarce resources like water and energy? And what if we could do it not only for companies, but also for a whole value chain? What if we could do it for a country?' Suddenly people started to realize that maybe we are far more than just a software company, and we can have a much bigger impact on the world than we have today."

This approach enabled SAP to enter new markets and new product categories without discrediting where they came from, but actually doing it in a way that enhanced who they were. SAP started to realise that while the company needed more than a facelift, it did not need a new heart.

This reinforcement of the company's purpose became the driver behind SAP's ambition to double its addressable market by entering three new product categories: mobile, cloud, and in-memory technology. In 2010 SAP had no revenue in any of those markets, and Hagemann Snabe and McDermott made it clear to everyone that they wanted to become number one in all three within five years. Mobile, cloud and in-memory technology were SAP's opportunity to scale its true value proposition and become a growth company again. The concept of ERP – enterprise resource planning – was at least as relevant as it had ever been. It just had to be delivered in a new way, on new platforms and through a new business model.

* * *

Today, a little more than six years after Hagemann Snabe and McDermott started the journey towards reinventing SAP, the results speak for themselves. By delivering double-digit growth every year since, SAP has turned itself into the world's fourth biggest software company and Germany's most valuable company. In five years both the top and the bottom line have doubled. Significantly 70% of the new revenue comes from products SAP did not have on the shelves five years ago.

In 2010 SAP was perceived as a slow-moving software dinosaur. Today the company is heavily involved in various exciting projects such as how DNA-analysis can make cancer treatments more effective, how seismic analysis can be used to discover new oil fields, and how

Formula 1 teams can improve decision making by collecting and interpreting real-time data faster.

The transformation of SAP shows what it takes for a company to stay at the top through re-inventing itself from a position of strength. If senior figures wait until the need for change is obvious it is already too late, and suddenly the company can find itself at the edge of the cliff next to Butch Cassidy and the Sundance Kid.

Keeping a successful company vibrantly alive takes a consistent and continuous assessment of the marketplace, the same type of assessment that was done when the company first came into existence.

Most successful companies look at the market and say: how can we protect our existing business? SAP looked at the market and asked a different question: is there a better and potentially more successful way of living out our purpose? If we didn't have a business to protect, how would we build one that reinforces what we are really all about?

By re-connecting to its reason for existing, SAP found the courage to break the business model that had served it so well for decades. The company became a living example that in a radically changing business landscape, there is only one way to protect yourself from disruption – do it yourself.

Principle #3:
Burn Your Trophies

Will the marathon ever be run in under two hours?

This thought-provoking teaser from an online ad triggered my professional curiosity and led me to attend a conference in London in 2014 where a group of scientists had come together to discuss where the limit of human endeavour lies.

John Hayes became the first official marathon world record holder by running 2:55:18 in 1905 but within 16 years 26 minutes had been shaved off his record. By the time I was collecting my name badge at the conference centre the world record was down to 2:03:07, almost 52 minutes faster than Hayes. As the moderator of the conference pointed out while introducing the first speaker, the best female athletes nowadays easily run a marathon 30 minutes quicker than Hayes and his compatriots a century or so ago.

However, the men's marathon world record has hit a plateau indicating that we may be close to the limits of physical performance. But how close are we to that ceiling? Is the current plateau a permanent one, or just a temporary flattening before the next breakthrough?

At the conference it quickly became apparent to me that there is no shortage of theories. After a panel debate about muscle fibre types, I fell into a conversation with a tall American professor in biomechanics who said that in comparison with other species humans are athletically disadvantaged by the size of our limbs. Having evolved from apes with big feet and plenty of muscle all the way up the leg we are naturally limited in terms of acceleration. In a 100m Olympic final with all animal species, Usain Bolt, the fastest man on the planet with a time of 9.58 sec, would come in 28th, the professor explained, just ahead of the elephant. The cheetah would win in around 5.55 sec.

A few hours later, in a break between two sessions, a Dutch mathematician looked sceptically at me when I asked him if the sub-two-hour marathon is possible within the next 50 years. "Look at how long it took to get from 2:16 to 2:12," he said and paused for a moment. "It took seven years. Going from 2:12 to 2:08 took almost 20 years, and from 2:08 to 2:03.23 (the world record in August 2014) another 29 years. I really struggle to see the world record improving much more."

* * *

It is not really breaking news that scientists question the potential limits of human endeavour. They have always done so. Nor is it breaking news that they are often wrong. Some scientists once believed that if a man ran a mile in less than four minutes, his lungs would explode, or that if a woman ran a marathon she might die.

In the early 1950s the world record for the mile seemed stuck at 4:01:4, and there was scientific consensus that getting below four minutes would be close to impossible. This assumption was strongly backed by the Australian John Landy who had run within three seconds of the barrier no fewer than six times in an 18-month period. Landy had become the poster boy for the impossibility of the four-minute-mile. As he was quoted saying: "The four-minute mile is a brick wall, and I shan't attempt it again".

But then on May 6 in 1954 a medical student from Oxford named Roger Bannister ran 3:59.4. The wall had fallen, and what happened six weeks later? John Landy, who had come so close to running a sub-four minute mile so many times without success went out and did it in 3:58.0! Today, more than 60 years later, that mile record stands at 3:43.13.

The Jamaican sprint phenomenon Usain Bolt is another example of someone who has forced the scientists back to the drawing board when it comes to the limits of human performance. At the Beijing Olympics in 2008 he smashed the 100m world record by running 9.69, despite slowing down during the last 10 metres to celebrate. According to a study by the Norwegian scientist Dr Hans Eriksen, had Bolt kept his speed all the way he would have run 9.55.

Before Bolt came along it was treated as a scientific truth that world class sprinters were compact and muscular. A study in the Journal of Sports Science and Medicine confirmed they ranged from 5ft 9in at the low end to 6ft 3in at the absolute max. Big guys tend to have physics working against them because they can't produce enough power to overcome the drag of a large body.

But then Bolt showed up. He was 6ft 5in and looked more like a basketball player than a sprinter, yet he was able to use his size as an extra engine rather than as a brake; a spidery giant whose legs generated the propulsive power of a cannonball-thighed running back. Because of his stride length he was able to run the 100m in 41 strides while most other sprinters do so in around 46.

Taking sprinting to a completely new level, Bolt reopened the question: how fast can human beings run? Are we actually much further from reaching the performance ceiling than we thought?

* * *

Both Bannister and Bolt teach us that records often feel and look like unbreakable barriers before they get broken.

When the golf player Jack Nicklaus was at his peak it was almost impossible to imagine a better player. Then Tiger Woods showed up and raised the bar even higher.

In the 1980s the tennis champion Martina Navratilova was perceived as a superhuman machine with an aggressiveness and power never seen in the sport before. By the late 90s the Williams sisters entered the stage, winning title after title with physiques that made Navratilova look like a slim teenager.

In baseball a 90 mph fastball used to be noteworthy. Today it is the access ticket to even be a part of the game.

In music the standard for what is possible has also been reset. As James Conlon, the renowned conductor of the Los Angeles Opera, puts it: "Pieces that were once considered too difficult for any but the very best musicians are now routinely played by conservatory students."

In almost every industry this is the case. When we think we have reached the top of the mountain someone comes along and shows us that what we thought was the peak was closer to the base camp.

There is no obvious reason why this rapid development will not continue. In 20 years most industries will look back at the standards of today and think they were absolutely average, the same way they today look back at the standards 20 years ago and are completely unimpressed. However, there still seems to be a natural resistance built into our psyche, something that at all times has made it difficult for us to accept that any existing barrier is likely to be broken.

Historically we see the same pattern repeat itself: pessimism followed by success. As far back as the first century AD the Roman engineer Julius Frontinus proclaimed: "Inventions have long-since reached their limit – and I see no hope for further developments." He was soon to be proved wrong.

Similarly, in 1837 the medicine professor Alfred Velpeau warned: "The abolition of pain in surgery is a chimera. It is absurd to go on seeking it…" Yet nine years later John Collins Warren made history with the first successful surgical procedure performed with anaesthesia.

In 1920 the New York Times dismissed the notion that a rocket could function in a vacuum. On 17 July 1969, the day after the launch of Apollo 11, the New York Times issued this correction with the words: "It is now definitely established that a rocket can function in a vacuum as well as in an atmosphere. The Times regrets the error."

The world is full of breakthroughs like Apollo 11. Glass, mirrors, anaesthesia, planes and computers all seemed like impossible dreams before they came into existence. But still, despite this endless list of evidence, why do human beings struggle to imagine the rapid barrier continuing to be broken? This is one of the greatest mysteries of the human psyche: what causes us to consistently underrate the potential of our endeavour?

* * *

Here are two questions to think about:

1) On a scale of 1-10*, by how much have your values, beliefs and preferences changed in the past 10 years?

2) On a scale of 1-10, by how much do you expect your values, beliefs and preferences to change in the next 10 years?

If you are like most people, you believe that you have changed much more in the past decade than you expect to in the forthcoming one. Obviously, you have already learned life's lessons.

This phenomenon is what Dan Gilbert, a psychology researcher at Harvard University, calls *the end of history*

---

* 1 = no change at all, 10 = drastic and complete change.

illusion. In Science Magazine in 2012 Gilbert and his team shared the results of a study in which they asked more than 19,000 people to complete personality and values assessments, either recalling how they'd changed in the last decade, or predicting how they would change in the next. This allowed Gilbert and his team to gain an insight into whether, for example, 40-year-olds looking backwards remember changing more than 30-year-olds looking forwards predict that they will change.

The results were thought provoking. No matter if Gilbert asked teenagers, the middle-aged, or seniors, the pattern was the same. Everyone believes that they have experienced significant personal growth and changes up to the present moment, but will not substantially do so again in the future. In all ages we tend to believe that who we are today is essentially who we will be tomorrow. We acknowledge that development is a process that's brought us to this particular moment in time, but now we're pretty much done. As Gilbert concluded: "Human beings are a work in progress that mistakenly thinks they are finished."

* * *

The end of history illusion is the reason why we struggle to imagine that the current limits in the field we work in can be pushed even further, just like we found it difficult to believe that anyone would ever break the four-minute-mile. There is a natural arrogance built into our psyche causing us to feel that wherever we find ourselves in life we believe that we are near the peak of our evolution.

Paradoxically, you find this view echoed by some of the most recognised experts and thinkers of all times.

In 1888 the renowned Canadian-American astronomer Simon Newcomb said: "We are probably nearing the limit of all we can know about astronomy." Two decades later Einstein launched his theory of relativity, which answered some of the major questions in physics and astronomy.

In his career as a physicist the respected William Thomson Kelvin rejected the possibility of flying machines as well as X-ray.

And when Boeing introduced its B247 model in 1933 Charles "Monty" Monteith, the chief engineer of the company, confidently said: "They'll never build'em any bigger." The B247 had room for 10 passengers, two pilots, and a stewardess. Today the world's largest passenger airliner, the A380, takes 900 passengers.

To top it all, in 1894 the American physicist Albert Michelson told his peers: "The more important fundamental laws and facts of physical science have all been discovered, and these are now so firmly established that the possibility of their ever being supplanted in consequence of new discoveries is exceedingly remote... Our future discoveries must be looked for in the sixth place of decimals."

Counterintuitively it turns out that experts often underestimate the potential for improvement within their fields. Sometimes it seems that the more successful and knowledgeable they are the more their outlook is influenced by *the end of history illusion.*

In a business context, this phenomenon is one of the biggest threats to a successful company. The more success an organisation has achieved the more likely it is to feel *we have found the recipe... our potential for further growth is limited... we have seen it all, we know it all... we have arrived.* Once this mind-set settles in and starts infecting the corporate culture it is the beginning of the end. You have then allowed *the end of history illusion* to extinguish your fire.

* * *

"Nokia, our platform is burning."

There was no way you could misinterpret the 1,300 word long *burning platform memo*, which in February 2011 landed in the inboxes of Nokia's 90,000 employees. No superfluous packaging, no excuses and no glaze on top to sweeten the message. Just the brutal truth. The sender was Nokia's new CEO Stephen Elop. A few months earlier, the Canadian software engineer and former Microsoft executive had been entrusted with the responsibility of restoring Nokia's prestige, the first non-Finn to be put in charge of the company. The board had lost patience with Olli-Pekka Kallasvuo, the man who confidently called the iPhone *nothing but a niche product.*

Elop's diagnosis of Nokia was gloomy. In his *burning platform memo* he compared the company to a man standing on an oil platform in the North Sea. The man was awakened abruptly by a massive explosion, which had set the entire oil platform on fire. Through the smoke and extreme heat he fought his way from his cabin to the platform to realize that he was trapped. As the flames drove him to the edge, he could see the cold, dark sea below him. He had only seconds to react: he could stay on the burning platform and be burnt alive by the flames, or he could plunge 30 metres into the freezing water.

Under normal circumstances, he would never have considered plunging, but these were not normal circumstances. It was a choice between certain death and a slim chance of survival. He decided to jump. Later he was rescued.

"We too, are standing on a burning platform, and we must decide how we are going to change our behaviour," wrote Elop, before he explained how Nokia was under attack in the high-end market from Apple, in the mid-end market from Android, and in the low-end market from Chinese manufacturers, who – as Elop noticed – were cracking out devices faster than the time it took Nokia to polish a PowerPoint presentation.

"We have more than one explosion – we have multiple points of scorching heat that are fuelling a blazing fire around us," he continued. "In fact, we poured gasoline on our own burning platform. We fell behind, we missed big trends, and we lost time. We now find ourselves years behind."

Then he pushed his finger directly into Nokia's most festering wound: the iPhone. "The first iPhone shipped in 2007, and we still don't have a product that is close to their experience. Unbelievable."

* * *

Stephen Elop's burning platform memo was a wake up call for Nokia, but even though the company improved under Elop's leadership it was too late to win back relevance. However, more interestingly, in 2004, before the iPhone even existed, Elop's legendary predecessor, Jorma Ollila, had actually delivered a very similar burning platform message to Nokia's employees.

Ollila had started to get nervous about a growing complacency in the company. He clearly wasn't imagining that Nokia's telecom business, which he had taken control of in 1992 and turned into one of the world's most recognized brands, would be left in tatters just six years later. But he had started to pick up early indications that the walls of its famous company culture were starting to crack.

In an interview in The Economist in June 2000 Olilla was asked what he thought was Nokia's biggest threat? Without hesitation he replied: complacency. During the upturn, thousands of new employees had been hired, people who had never seen anything other than success at Nokia. The collective memory of the early 90s when the company found itself in life-threatening circumstances and standing on the edge of the abyss had become weaker and weaker. People were taking success for granted. Privileges had turned into rights, and it made Ollila uncomfortable. Therefore, he decided to tour Nokia's branches throughout the world with the message that it was necessary to work harder, be humble, and show more respect for competitors.

Ollila's favourite example, which he would use to fire

up the troops, was Nokia's famous and almost sacred production and development centres in the small town of Salo, a half-hour drive from Helsinki. When Ollila came to visit at 3pm, the parking lot in Salo was often half empty. It made him furious. "What are you doing? We are competing against the South Koreans (Samsung), they are ahead of us on technology, their implementation is extremely rapid, and they work 14 hours a day, six days a week. You arrive at the office at 9am and leave again at 3pm. How on earth do you imagine being able to beat them with that level of effort? Do you really think that we are competing against second-rate engineers?" he thundered.

* * *

Ollila's attempt to shake up the culture of Nokia was theoretically correct. The perception that *we have reached the top of the mountain* kills the hunger to improve in any organisation. As Ollila later described in his 450-page memoir: "Lack of cash is the worst thing that can happen to a company but the second worst is lots of success. It makes you believe you have found the golden path, one you can always revert to if you need to."

However, in real life Nokia never really took the message to heart. While Ollila preached humility and respect for competitors, when Anssi Vankoji, the head of Nokia's mobile phones, was asked if he felt threatened by the fact that Nokia's rival BenQ had bought Siemens' handset business, he replied, "two turkeys do not make an eagle".

Across the board Ollila was fighting an exhausting

battle against *the end of history illusion,* which had spread like a virus among Nokia's troops. He could preach about the right attitudes to exhaustion, but as long as the bottom line looked healthy, his words were only met with the reaction: "Look at the numbers. We are the best in the business, so why change?"

Injecting urgency into a successful company is a tough task. Natural forces tend to push us toward stability and contentment. As the American management professor, John Kotter, has put it: "Urgency leads to success, success leads to complacency."

Contrary to Elop seven years later, Ollila didn't have a burning platform to help him drive the urgency for improvement and change. Nokia year 2004 was not forced to plunge 30 meters from a platform into the freezing water in order to survive. The company was practically printing money, and this is probably the single biggest management challenge in successful organisations: how do you convince people who perceive themselves as best in class that they are nowhere near their limit? How do you ignite a fire when there is no burning platform in sight?

* * *

While I travelled back home on the tube after having spent the day with scientists at the conference in London I began to reflect on what I had heard. One lesson seemed to stand out: it is impossible to predict the potential of human endeavour without first understanding the nature of our limitations. Before we can answer the question "Will a human being ever run a sub-two-hour-marathon?" we have to deal with a different question: *what actually makes us slow down?*

During the conference it had become pretty clear to me that while the scientists disagreed on many aspects of endurance performance, there was a fairly broad consensus about what prevents human beings from going faster. This is built upon the assumption that the cardiovascular system has a limited capacity to supply oxygen to the active muscles during intense exercise. As a result, skeletal muscle oxygen demand outstrips supply, causing the onset of lactic acid production, ultimately making us slow down. This is why the most important effect of any intervention that improves performance, be it training, nutritional interventions or drug use, is to change oxygen delivery to, and oxygen utilization by, the active muscles during exercise.

It is the cardiovascular endurance model that drives how elite athletes train in their pursuit to push the boundaries. At the same time it is the model that makes scientists doubt if a human being will ever be able to run a marathon in under two hours. Seen through the lens of the cardiovascular endurance model, the human engine is pretty much optimized, and as a consequence, records will not *leap* forward, but inch forward incrementally. World records will become more and more infrequent, and eventually no longer be broken.

In other words, if the sub-two-hour-marathon is ever going to become a reality the breakthrough has to come from a new perspective, a different way of looking at the question: what makes us slow down?

This is where Samuele Marcora, an Italian-born exercise physiologist at the University of Kent comes into the picture. The first time I came across him was four years ago when I was researching for a book (The Gold Mine Effect) and writing about *talent clusters*. Marcora is the man behind one of the most intriguing pieces of research in sports science over the past couple of decades, which has the potential to re-shape the way we think about athletic potential.

* * *

The question Marcora asks is one that makes the disciples of the cardiovascular endurance model confused: what if it is actually our brain, and not our body, that makes us slow down?

In one of his best-known studies Marcora tested his thesis on elite athletes. The study had two phases. First, Marcora put a group of fit athletes on stationary bikes and asked them to ride to complete exhaustion at around 90% of their VO2 max. Usually they would reach this point after around 12 minutes. Immediately afterwards Marcora then asked the athletes to do a maximum power test, where they push themselves as hard as possible for five seconds.

It turned out that the athletes produced three times as much power in those five seconds than at any point during the 12 minutes. As Marcora has put it: "Really, it was the most obvious demonstration of the fact that fatigue is not physiological. If our limit was physiological the athletes wouldn't be able to triple their output power without recovery and just after having pushed themselves to complete exhaustion."

This research is potentially game-changing, because it proves what other studies have been indicating too; fatigue is a multifactorial phenomenon, a combination of psychological and physiological factors, but the brain seems to play a bigger role than we have previously thought.

In another set of studies, which Marcora published in Frontiers of Human Neuroscience in 2014, he revealed how athletes on bikes who saw messages of happy faces rode on average 13 per cent longer than those who were shown unhappy faces. Subliminal words like 'go' and 'lively' also reduced the perception of effort and improved performance by seventeen per cent over downbeat messages like 'toil' and 'sleep'. As Marcora explained: "Something unique was happening inside their heads, a brain adaptation. Their perception of effort became far lower."

It leaves us with several truly thought provoking questions: could the body be pushed much further if only the brain would let it happen? If we deeply understand how our brains control fatigue, can we then intervene and manipulate it to let the body go faster for longer?

On the bottom line the message is clear. It feels as if it is the body which gives up, but it is actually the brain – yet as long as we are stuck solely in the cardiovascular endurance model we will not be able to access its full power.

* * *

The idea that our brain, not only our body, is a limiting factor for pushing athletic performance to the next level is not only interesting in a sporting context. On a more philosophical level it also holds a key lesson: if you want to change people's idea about what is possible you need to change the paradigm they see the world through.

Every paradigm comes with a set of assumptions and beliefs. When sport scientists question whether anyone will ever run a marathon in under two hours it is because their paradigm (the cardiovascular endurance model) is built on an assumption about what makes athletes slow down. As long as we believe the limiting factor is solely the cardiovascular system a sub-two-hour-marathon seems very far away. But if we start seeing the world through a different paradigm, as Marcora suggests, in which the brain is the limiting factor, we suddenly see an opportunity for improvement.

This is the sort of paradigm shift it takes to override *the end of history illusion*. When we are stuck with a set of assumptions that makes us believe that we have reached the top of the mountain we need someone to offer us a new perspective that says... *this is not the top of the mountain. Actually, it is just a small hill, because the real mountain to climb is up here.*

For years management literature has spoken about using a burning platform to drive change and improvement. But burning platform psychology rarely works in a successful company. That's why Ollila's battle against complacency in Nokia failed. You can't set the platform on fire if your matches are wet from being soaked in success.

To push a successful organisation to new heights you need to inspire people. You need to re-think your potential by changing perspective and the lens you use to look at the world through.

* * *

The results Lego has delivered are almost second to none. When CEO Jorgen Vig Knudstorp presented Lego's result in early 2015 it was the tenth consecutive year of record profits. Over the past 10 years, the total toy market in USA has dropped by 9%, but without Lego's growth it would have been down by 16%. This has made Lego the world's most valuable toy manufacturer.

This dominance draws a picture of a company that has more than enough reason to go celebrating itself from morning to night, but this does not happen. Instead Knudstrop is deliberately trying to eliminate any symptoms of *end of history thinking* in Lego.

Having presented his tenth consecutive record result he decided to stand up in front his team to challenge them: "Congratulations, you have delivered a great result, but are you actually so sure that we are competing in the toy industry after all?" Knudstorp began.

"Imagine if a 12 year old boy did not buy Lego, what do you think he would then buy instead? Would he buy another toy, for example Megablocks, or one of the other traditional players in our industry? Or would he rather buy an iPhone or an FC Barcelona football jersey?

Let's assume that he bought an iPhone. What does that mean? Well, it means that Lego's battlefield is no longer the toy industry, now the battlefield is the children's playroom. This changes the picture completely because in the children's playroom our main competitor is not Megablocks. It is Apple, and when we start comparing ourselves to a company that has achieved the growth that Apple has, Lego has a lot of potential for improvement. It actually makes us look like a beginner again."

Framing the need for innovation through that lens has inspired Lego to invest heavily in ethnographic studies of how kids around the world really play. For example, the research has shown that kids no longer make meaningful distinctions between digital play and physical play, a phenomenon Lego calls *One Reality*, which led the company to start creating hybrid digital-physical experiences. For example, Lego has launched Lego Fusion, where kids build a model of a house or castle, take a photo of it with a tablet, and watch their creations become part of a virtual world inside an accompanying app.

Another example of how Lego tries to expand its market by bridging the gap between the physical and digital world is the major success *Lego Dimensions*, a toy-to-life action-adventure videogame for PlayStation and Xbox that merges physical Lego brick building with interactive console gameplay.

By changing the way it looks at the market Lego has re-thought its own potential and realised that although the company is already unbelievable successful, Lego is still not anywhere close to its limit. As Knudstorp has put it: "It's about discovering what's obviously Lego, but has never been seen before."

* * *

Knudstorp is trying to solve one of the toughest management challenges: how do you keep raising the bar and drive such a successful organisation to new heights? And he is doing it by re-framing the way Lego looks at the market. This re-framing overrides *the end of history illusion* because it completely changes Lego's perception about its potential, just as Samuele Marcora's reframe changes our idea about how fast humans can run a marathon. Suddenly you are not a fat cat that has reached the top of the mountain. You are now a small energetic entrepreneur who is going out there to conquer the world.

Coca Cola did something similar after it won the battle against Pepsi and went on to dominate the soft-drink industry for more than 50 years. With such a dominance it can be difficult to see where growth can possibly come from. However, the management team took a step back and started to look at the company from a new perspective: "A 50% market share in the soft drinks industry is great, but do we compete in that industry after all? What if we actually compete in the industry for all liquids that can go into the human body? In that case our market share is tiny, and suddenly we are back to being a small entrepreneur again ready to attack the market."

This fresh perspective inspired Coca Cola to move into new markets, for example the production of filtered water. Today Coca Cola's water brands Dasani and Smartwater are among the world's biggest.

This is what great leaders do to override *the end*

of history illusion. They make the world bigger and themselves smaller. They reframe reality to create a benchmark that makes them look like a beginner, and they work to *find* competition instead of fleeing from it, all with the purpose of fabricating urgency and a constructive dissatisfaction with the status quo. This is the counter-intuitive nature of keeping a successful organisation hungry. You must strive to be number one, but you can never truly get there.

* * *

Three weeks after the conference in London I saw that the Kenyan runner Dennis Kimetto had shaved another 26 seconds off the world record winning the 2014 Berlin Marathon in 2 hours 2 minutes and 57 seconds. The human species had moved one step closer to the sub-two-hour mark.

The Next Nokia
Could Be You

Economists often use the term *The Third Generation Curse* to describe how family-owned businesses squander their wealth. As the saying goes: from shirtsleeves to shirtsleeves in three generations.

The first generation – the founders – know every brick of the foundation. Having built the company in the first place they know what inspired it and the sacrifices it took to make it successful. Their mindset is to pay attention to every customer interaction, the attitude of each employee and every dollar spent.

The second generation inherits the business and holds it all together. They have a clear memory of the long and hard work it took to build the company's success and so grow the business with a healthy mix of humility and confidence.

Then, so the theory goes, the kids of the second generation come along and slowly squander it all. They do not understand the blood, sweat and tears invested in accumulating the wealth – all they have ever seen is success and they expect it to automatically continue as if it was a human right.

This gradual change in attitude is a key reason why only 12% of family businesses survive the third generation. However, the underlying logic of the third generation curse applies more widely. As we have seen with Nokia, when any organisation loses its memory of the tough times, people often start to think success will never end. Because all the swans they have seen are white, they assume black swans do not exist. Confidence morphs into arrogance, and as a consequence they disregard the risk of disruption.

Even a company as successful and dominant as Lego faces the threat of the third generation curse. 15 years ago it was on the edge of bankruptcy. However, today the memory of that life-threatening crisis is fading. Very few of the current employees worked for Lego back then. The rest have never experienced Lego being anything but overwhelmingly successful. This is how years of success breed the illusion of continuity: the fundamental assumption that drive successful companies into complacency.

My hope is that the principles presented in this book have given the reader the insights and tools to defeat it. It is a demanding battle to win. As we have learned, human nature can be counterproductive to remaining successful. Successful companies are fighting inbuilt psychological biases that work, often without them realizing it, like a powerful magnet naturally pulling them towards the status quo. To *de-bias* ourselves takes a consistent effort and a willingness to confront ourselves with questions like:

1. How can we get better at untangling skill and luck in our business?
2. If we were to question success with the same scepticism as failure, what questions would we then need to ask which are not being asked at present?
3. What *leading performance indicators* in our business do we need to increase our focus on in order to identify problems *before* they become obvious?
4. If we got sacked tomorrow and the board appointed a new management team without the emotional investment in what worked in the past, what do we think the new leadership would do?
5. Are we protecting our core purpose or are we obsessed with protecting the physical manifestation of how we make money?
6. If we were certain that our core business would be significantly changed or maybe even completely gone within the next three to five years, what should we do today?
7. How can we re-frame our market so that we make ourselves look like a beginner again?

I appreciate that, despite the examples presented in this book, it may still be difficult for successful companies to imagine a world where they no longer play a pivotal role. That's human nature. However, there is one thing I am certain of: if it can happen to Nokia it can happen to you too.

Acknowledgements

Some authors claim they produce their best work by going into self-imposed exile in a lonely loft cut off from the rest of the world. Several months later they return with a finished book.

For me, isolation doesn't work. Whenever I decide to write a book I have a lot more questions than answers. The answers grow and mature in the process of researching. They are being shaped by the people I meet on my journey and by the organisations I work with. To do good work I depend on getting feedback along the way and being challenged by sharp brains.

This book is no exception, and therefore I would like to thank everyone who has helped shape the concept of *Hunger in Paradise*. Thanks to all those who during one of my lectures asked a critical question that got me to re-think a message. Thanks to those who shared an experience and a new perspective.

In particular, I would like to thank my editor Sean Ingle for his honest feedback and constant reminders that the reader is the most important person. And Henrik Hyldgaard, my good friend, co-author and usual sparring partner, who has kept pushing the bar for this book with his sense of uniqueness and clarity of concept.

Last but not least I would like to thank my closest family for the tolerance they have shown me along the way. I appreciate that it is not necessarily the easiest thing in the world to be around an author with a challenging deadline.

Notes

From Greatness to Irrelevance

Development in human life expectancy. *UN's World Population Prospects.* 2015.

Development in corporate life expectancy. *Innosight Executive Briefing Richard N. Foster.* 2012.

The Flipside of Human Nature

Intomobile.com. *Nokia's CEO Kallasvuo says Apple iPhone is a niche product.* April 17, 2008.

Principle #1:
Never Trust Success

Analytical Football. *How Well Does Goal Differential Explain Points?* www.analyticalfootball.blogspot.com, 2009.

Anderson, Chris and David Sally. *The Number Game: Why Everything You Know About Soccer Is Wrong.* Penguin Books, 2013.

Cleary, Paul. *Too much luck.* Black Inc., 2011.

Dixon, Marc J and Stuart G. Coles. *Modelling Association Football Scores and Inefficiencies in the Football Betting Market. Journal of the Royal Statistical Society.* Series C (Applied Statistics) Vol. 46, No. 2 (1997), pp. 265-280.

Galton, Francis: *Regression Towards Mediocrity in Hereditary Stature.* The Journal of the Anthropological Institute of Great Britain and Ireland, Vol. 15 (1886), pp. 246-263.

Gilovich, Thomas. How We Know What Isn't So: *The Fallibility of Human Reason in Everyday Life*. Free Press, 1993.

Groysberg, Boris. *Chasing Stars: The Myth of Talent and the Portability of Performance*. Princeton University Press, 2012.

Kahneman, Daniel. *Thinking Fast and Slow*. Farrar, Straus and Giroux, 2013.

Kuper, Simon and Stefan Szymanski. *Soccernomics*. Nation Books, 2012.

Langer, Ellen and Jane Roth. *Heads I win, tails it's chance: The illusion of control as a function of the sequence of outcomes in a purely chance task*. Journal of Personality and Social Psychology, Vol 32(6), Dec 1975, 951-955.

Lunde, Niels. *Miraklet på LEGO*. JP/Politikens Forlag, 2013.

Mauboussin, Michael. *The Success Equation: Untangling Skill and Luck in Business, Sports, and Investing*. Harvard Business Review Press, 2012.

Odeon, Terrance: *Do Investors Trade Too Much?* University of California, Berkeley - Haas School of Business, April 1998.

Reichheld, Fred and Rob Markey. *The Ultimate Question 2.0 (Revised and Expanded Edition): How Net Promoter Companies Thrive in a Customer-Driven World*. Harvard Business Review Press, 2011.

Rosenzweig, Phil. *The Halo Effect: … and the Eight Other Business Delusions That Deceive Managers*. Free Press, 2009.

Schiff, Peter. *The Real Crash: America's Coming Bankruptcy: How to Save Yourself and Your Country*. St. Martin's Press, 2012.

Taylor, Mark. *The Power of Goals* - www.thepowerofgoals.blogspot. com.

Telegraph. *Newcastle United manager Alan Pardew fighting to keep his job following Liverpool thrashing at St James' Park*. April 27, 2013.

UEFA Statistics – www.uefa.com.

Principle #2:
If It Ain't broke, Consider Breaking it

Bazerman, Max H. and Ann E. Tenbrunsel. *Blind Spots: Why We Fail to Do What's Right and What to Do about It.* Princeton University Press, 2012.

Bazerman, Max H and Don A. Moore. *Judgment in Managerial Decision Making.* Wiley, 2008.

Christensen, Clayton. *The Innovator's Dilemma: The Revolutionary Book That Will Change the Way You Do Business.* Harper Business, 2011.

Grove, Andrew. *Only The Paranoid Survive: How to Exploit the Crisis Points That Challenge Every Company.* Crown Business, 1999.

Jyske Bank TV. *Er Creative Destruction vejen ud af den økonomiske krise?* April, 2013.

McCraw, Thomas K. *Prophet of Innovation: Joseph Schumpeter and Creative Destruction.* Harvard University Press, 2010.

Tedlow, Richard. *Denial: Why Business Leaders Fail to Look Facts in the Face – and What to Do About it.* Portfolio Hardcover, 2010.

Lakhani, Karim R., Marco Iansiti, and Noah Fisher. *SAP 2014: Reaching for the Cloud.* Harvard Business School Case 614-052, January 2014.

Principle #3:
Burn Your Trophies

Costa, Gabriel and Michael R. Huber and John T. Saccoman. *Understanding Sabermetrics: An Introduction to the Science of Baseball Statistics.* McFarland, 2007.

Häjkiö, Martti. *Nokia: The Inside Story.* Financial Times. Prentice Hall, 2002.

The Wall Street Journal. Full Text: *Nokia CEO Stephen Elop's 'Burning Platform' Memo.* February 9, 2011.

Conference Paper: *The Effect of Mental Fatigue on Long-Term Endurance Performance.* Chiara Gattoni, Barry V O'Neil, Federico Schena, Samuele M Marcora. 2016.

Article: *The Central Governor Model of Exercise Regulation Teaches Us Precious Little about the Nature of Mental Fatigue and Self-Control Failure.* Michael Inzlicht, Samuele Marcora. 2016.

Martin, K.A. and Hall, C.R. *Using mental imagery to enhance intrinsic Motivation.* Journal of Sport and Exercise Psychology, 1995.

Samuele M., Marcora, W.S. and Manning, V. *Mental fatigue impairs physical performance in humans.* Applied Physiology, 2009.

Amann, M., Hopkins, W.G. and Marcora, S.M. *Similar sensitivity of time to exhaustion and time-trial time to changes in endurance.* Medical Science Sports Exercise, 2008.

Marcora, S.M., Bosio, A. and de Morree, H.M. *Locomotor muscle fatigue increases cardiorespiratory responses and reduces performance during intense cycling exercise independently from metabolic stress.* Journal of Applied Physiology, 2008.

Quoidbach, Jordi; Gilbert, Daniel T.; Wilson, Timothy D. (2013-01-04). *The end of history illusion.* Science. 339 (6115): 96–98.

Tierney, John (2013-01-04). *You Won't Stay the Same, Study Finds.* The New York Times, 2013-10-09.

Gilbert, Daniel. *The psychology of your future self.* TED.com, 14 May 2016